Food

542447

641 (E)

Why do we need food?

All living things need food to stay alive and healthy.
Your body needs to take in many different substances
in order to grow and to keep working properly.
You get these substances by eating different foods.

Our bodies are made up of millions
of tiny living units called *cells*.
These foods supply the substances
our bodies need to make new cells
and to repair damaged cells.

These foods supply the energy
our bodies need to keep working
properly.

These foods help to keep our bodies
healthy, and to stop us getting
certain diseases.

These foods help to keep us warm,
and also to supply us with energy.

Where does food come from?

Animals get their food from plants or other animals.
Some animals, such as cows and sheep, eat only plants.
Animals which eat only plants are called *herbivores*.

Some animals, such as lions and tigers, eat
other animals. Animals which eat other animals
are called *carnivores*.

Human beings eat plants
and animals. People used to
get food from animals
by hunting them. Today,
we get food from animals
by raising them on farms.

We get food from plants
by growing crops.
The wheat in this field
can be made into flour.
The flour can be used
to make bread, and other foods.

3

Food and energy

Your body needs power, or *energy*, to keep working.
Every time you move a muscle, you use energy.
Even when you are sitting down, you are using energy.
The muscles which keep your heart beating
and which make you breathe are using energy.
Your brain is using energy too.

Different types of food contain different amounts
of energy. Scientists used to measure the amount
of energy that a food contains in units called *calories*
(or *kilocalories*). Now, units called *kilojoules* are used.
One kilocalorie equals 4.18 kilojoules.

The diagram shows the amount of energy
found in one gram of various foods.

Cabbage 1 kilojoule   Apple 1.8 kilojoules   Milk 3.0 kilojoules

Baked beans 3.8 kilojoules   Beef sausages 9.0 kilojoules

Bread 10.0 kilojoules   Cheese 18.0 kilojoules   Butter 33.0 kilojoules

How much energy do people need?

Different people use up different amounts of energy.
The amount of energy you need depends on your age,
your sex, and the amount of work you do. In general,
males need more energy than females. Teenagers
and adults need more energy than very young children
and old people. People such as labourers,
whose jobs involve lots of physical work,
need more energy than office workers.

Three-year-old boys and girls
need about 4500 kilojoules a day.

A 15-year-old girl needs 13 000
kilojoules a day, but a 15-year-old
boy needs 15 000.

A patient lying in a hospital bed
needs only about 7 500 kilojoules a day.

A labourer on a building site
needs about 20 000 kilojoules a day.

A female clerk needs about 10 000
kilojoules a day, but a male clerk
needs about 12 000.

An old person needs only 8 500
kilojoules a day.

Different kinds of food

Carbohydrates

We get a lot of the energy we need from foods
which contain the substances known as *carbohydrates*.
Carbohydrates are made by plants, and contain carbon,
hydrogen and oxygen.

Carbohydrates take the form of either sugars
or starches. Some foods consist entirely of carbohydrates,
such as the sugar we put on cereals or in our tea.
Other foods consist only partly of carbohydrates.
We get starch in foods such as bread, cereals, rice
and potatoes. Our bodies turn the starch into sugars.
The sugars then combine with oxygen in the body,
and this gives us our energy.

Fats

We also get energy from foods which contain
the substances known as *fats*. We get most of our fats
from milk, butter and cheese, from margarine and
vegetable oils, and from the fat on meat. Nuts contain
a large amount of fat. In addition to providing us
with energy, fats help to keep us warm. But if you eat
more fats than your body can use up, you will put on
weight!

Proteins

The cells in your body are always working. So,
after a time, cells wear out, and need replacing.
New cells are made with the substances called *proteins*.
Proteins contain nitrogen, as well as carbon, hydrogen
and oxygen.

Meat and fish are two kinds of food which contain
plenty of proteins. There are also many proteins
in certain animal products, such as milk, cheese
and eggs. Proteins found in animal products are known
as *animal proteins*. Certain plant foods, such as peas,
soya beans and peanuts, also contain proteins.
Proteins found in plant foods are called *vegetable
proteins*.

Soya beans are a very important source of proteins.
It costs less to grow soya beans to provide proteins
than it does to get proteins from meat and fish.
So people in many countries get the proteins they need
by eating soya beans.

In our bodies, the proteins we eat are broken down
into chemicals called *amino-acids*. These chemicals
are then used to make new cells.

Testing for different foods

You can find out whether a food contains fat or starch
by these simple experiments.

Testing for starch
Add a few drops of the chemical
known as *iodine solution*
to the food. If a dark blue
or black colour is made,
the food contains starch.

Testing for fat
Rub or pour some food
onto a piece of blotting paper.
Let the paper dry.
If a greasy mark is left,
the food contains fat.

Vitamins

Many foods contain small amounts of chemical substances
called *vitamins*. These substances are known by certain
letters of the alphabet – especially A, B, C, D, E and K.
Vitamins help to keep you healthy. If you do not get enough
vitamins, you can become ill.

Certain foods, such as eggs, contain several
different vitamins. Other foods, like honey,
contain only one vitamin. Foods which are good sources
of vitamins are: liver, eggs, wholemeal bread, fruit
and vegetables.

Most people get enough vitamins by eating a variety
of different foods. Some people take vitamin pills
to make sure that they have enough vitamins each day.
But you can poison yourself if you have too much
vitamin A or vitamin D.

Vitamin A
Vitamin A is found in many foods
including milk, butter, cheese,
eggs, liver and margarine.
If you do not get enough vitamin A,
your skin becomes hard,
and the tissue of the eyes
may be damaged.

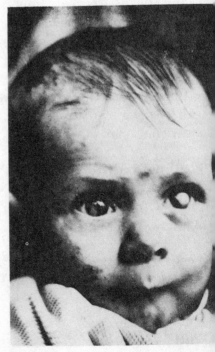

Vitamin B

Vitamin B is found in many foods
such as eggs, liver, kidney, yeast,
whole-grain cereals and some vegetables.
Vitamin B helps you to keep your skin
and nerves healthy. People who do not
get enough vitamin B may get a disease
called *beri-beri*, which affects
the nerves of your body.

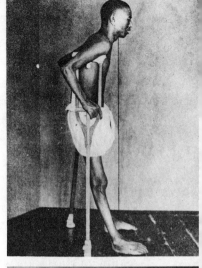

Vitamin C

People who do not get enough vitamin C
may develop a painful disease called
scurvy. In the past, many sailors
developed scurvy on long voyages,
because they did not have any fresh
fruit and vegetables to eat. The chief
sources of vitamin C are fruits, such as
oranges, lemons and blackcurrants,
and green vegetables.

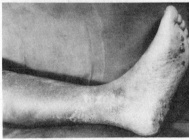

Vitamin D

Vitamin D helps to keep your bones
and teeth healthy. Children who do not
get enough vitamin D may develop
a bone disease called *rickets*. The bones
become weak and soft, and get bent easily.
Vitamin D is found in milk, eggs and
fish liver oils. Your body also makes
its own vitamin D. When bright sunlight
shines on your skin, certain substances
in the skin are changed into vitamin D.
So vitamin D is sometimes called
the 'sunshine vitamin'.

Minerals

Your body needs small amounts of about 20 different kinds of minerals. Minerals are needed to make blood, teeth and bones. You also need minerals to help make your nerves and muscles work properly.

Calcium

Your bones and teeth are hard, because they contain a mineral called *calcium*. If you do not get enough calcium, your teeth and bones will not form properly. Some of the foods which contain calcium are: cheese, cabbage, herrings, milk and bread.

Iron

You need iron to keep your blood healthy. If you do not get enough iron, you may suffer from a condition called *anaemia*. You look pale, and get tired very easily. The doctor may give you iron tablets to take.

A woman needs extra iron when she is going to have a baby, so doctors often give a pregnant woman iron tablets to take.

Fibre

Fibre is a mixture of plant substances.
Your body needs plenty of foods containing fibre,
because fibre helps you to get rid of solid waste,
and to keep your bowels healthy. These foods also
fill you up without making you fat.

The main foods which contain fibre are: bread,
cereals, vegetables, fruit and nuts. Green, leafy
vegetables contain large amounts of fibre.
Food which contains large amounts of fibre
is sometimes called 'roughage'.

Fibre in bread

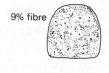

9% fibre

Wholemeal bread contains 9% fibre.

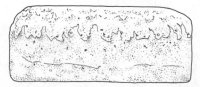
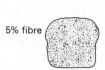

5% fibre

Brown bread contains 5% fibre.

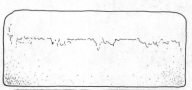
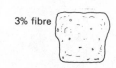

3% fibre

White bread contains 3% fibre.

A balanced diet

To keep fit and healthy, you must eat the right foods.
Every day, you should eat some body-building foods
(proteins), as well as some energy-giving foods
(carbohydrates and fats). You should also eat
some fresh fruit and vegetables, to give you vitamins
and fibre. These foods will also give you small amounts
of minerals. So if you eat several different foods,
you will get all the minerals your body needs.

The right amounts

In Britain, a lot of people eat too much.
Many adults eat about half a tonne of food a year.
This is more than your body needs.

   Often, people eat too much starch and sugar.
These are foods which give you energy. But if your body
does not use up the energy, then the energy is stored
as fat. The amount of energy you get from your food
should be exactly the same as the amount of energy
you use up.

   When you eat the right amount of food, and several
different foods, you are eating a 'balanced diet'.

Many people are overweight
because they eat too much,
and do not take enough exercise.
It is unhealthy to be overweight.
People who are overweight
are more likely to get ill.

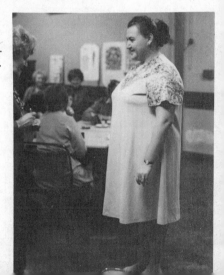

Slimming

Overweight people often try to lose weight, or *slim*. When you try to slim, you still need to eat a balanced diet. Your body still has to work properly. When you go on a slimming diet, you cut down on only those foods which contain fats and carbohydrates – the energy-giving foods. You actually eat less energy-giving food than you need. When you move, your body then has to use the energy which it has stored away as fat. The extra layers of fat in your body gradually get used up.

Slimming diets suggest that you cut down on certain foods. You are advised to avoid foods which contain large amounts of sugar, such as sweets, chocolates, cakes and biscuits. Most diets also tell you to cut down on fatty foods, such as chips and other fried foods. Instead, the diets advise you to eat foods like meat, fish, eggs and cheese, which contain plenty of proteins.

It is very important to see your doctor, before you go on a slimming diet. You should not try to lose weight too quickly, and you must not stop eating altogether. If you do stop eating, you will make yourself ill.

Water

About 70% of your body is water. Most of your blood
is water. Your cells also consist mainly of water,
and the spaces around the cells are filled with
a substance containing water.

Water has no energy value, but your body needs water
even more than food. You could live for several weeks
without food, but you would live for only a few days
without water.

All the time, your body is losing water.
Every time you breathe out, you lose a small amount
of water in your breath. You lose water when you sweat,
and when you go to the toilet.

Your body needs up to 2 litres of water a day
to replace the water it loses. You get this water
by eating as well as drinking. Many foods consist
mainly of water. Meat is 70% water. Vegetables
and fruit are mostly water. Potatoes are 90% water,
and tomatoes are 95% water.

Drinking water

Our drinking water is made clean enough to drink
by putting in chemicals to kill any germs. In many parts
of the country, a mineral called *fluoride* is also added
to the water, because fluoride helps to stop our teeth
from decaying.

Water which comes from springs often contains
more minerals than tap water, and is therefore known as
mineral water. Some people prefer to buy bottles
of mineral water to drink, rather than drink tap water.

What happens to the food you eat?

Inside your body, the food which you have eaten has to be changed, before it can be used to produce energy, and to make new cells. The food is broken down into small pieces, and turned into the substances which your body needs. The way in which the body breaks down food is called *digestion*.

In your mouth

The process of digestion begins in your mouth. Your sharp front teeth bite and tear the food into small chunks. Then your back teeth chew the food into smaller pieces.

At the same time, a liquid in your mouth starts to break down some of the food. This liquid is called *saliva*. Saliva contains a chemical which changes starch into sugar. Chemicals which help to change one substance into another are known as *enzymes*.

When you swallow food, it passes down a tube which runs from your throat into your stomach. This tube is called the *oesophagus*. Food takes about six seconds to travel down the oesophagus and reach your stomach.

In your stomach

Your stomach is like a big bag, which can expand
to let in all the food you swallow. In your stomach,
the food is broken down further. Special enzymes
help to change the food into the substances
which your body needs.

Food stays in your stomach for different lengths
of time. Bread and pastry can be broken down quickly,
but fat takes much longer to break down. Some foods
stay in your stomach for six hours.

Food passes from your stomach into a part
of your body called the *intestines*. Your intestines
consist of two parts, known as the *small* intestine
and the *large* intestine.

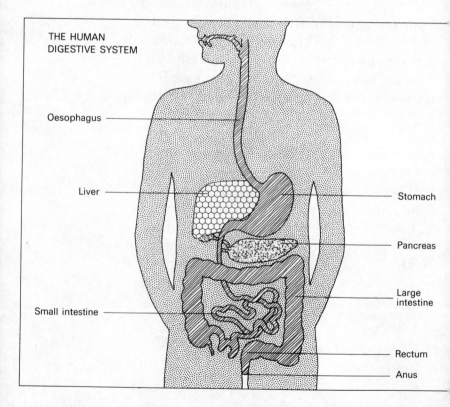

THE HUMAN
DIGESTIVE SYSTEM

Oesophagus

Liver

Small intestine

Stomach

Pancreas

Large
intestine

Rectum

Anus

In your intestines

In the small intestine, the process of digestion
carries on. More enzymes are used, many of these coming
from a part of your body called the *pancreas*.
The food which your body can use passes into your blood
through the wall of the small intestine. Your blood
carries this food to the various parts of your body,
where it is used to make energy, and to build new cells.

The food which has not been digested
passes into the large intestine. Here, water and salts
are taken out of the food. The solid waste that is left
is then pushed into the part of the body known as
the *rectum*. Finally, it passes out of the body
through the *anus*.

Your liver

Your blood carries some of the digested food
from the intestines to your liver. The liver changes
the food again, so that it can be used, or stored,
by your body. The liver also helps to protect you
from any poisons which might enter your body.

Your kidneys

Some waste substances are carried to the kidneys
by the blood. The kidneys produce a fluid called *urine*
from these waste substances. Urine passes to the bladder,
and then out of the body.

Cooking and preserving food

Many foods, such as meat and fish, need to be cooked
before we eat them. In these foods there are many germs,
or *bacteria*. Cooking kills the bacteria in the food.
If the food was not cooked properly, it could make us ill.

Cooking also softens food, and makes it easier
to chew and digest. Uncooked potatoes and flour
contain a lot of starch, which our bodies cannot
digest easily. So we cook potatoes to make them softer,
and we bake flour into bread, which is easier to digest.

But some foods can be cooked for too long.
When you cook vegetables for too long, you destroy
the vitamin C in them.

Keeping food fresh

Most foods can go bad very quickly. So it is important
to store foods properly. The air contains germs,
such as bacteria and moulds, which can make food decay.
This is why foods must be kept wrapped or covered.
Many foods will stay fresh longer, if they are stored
in a refrigerator.

Your hands often have harmful germs on them.
So you should always wash your hands
before touching food. The surfaces where food is put
must be kept clean. Your pots and pans must be clean too.
So it is important to do the washing-up properly!

Preserving food

Today, a lot of food which we eat is not fresh.
Often, the food has been treated in special ways so that
it will not go bad. When we use special methods to stop
food from going bad, we are *preserving* food.

Canning

Food is often preserved in tins, or in bottles
which have been specially sealed. The food is mixed
with water, put in the tin, and boiled. This cooks
the food, and kills any germs. The tin is then sealed,
so that no air or germs can get in. As long as the tin
is not opened, the food stays free from germs.
Food can be kept in tins for many years.

Freezing

Many foods can be preserved by freezing them.
Freezing does not kill any bacteria in the food,
but while food stays frozen, bacteria cannot grow.

Frozen foods can be kept for long periods.
But bacteria start to grow again, as soon as the food
thaws. So frozen foods must be cooked properly
before we eat them.

Drying

Many foods can be preserved by drying them,
to remove their water. Bacteria need water to live,
so dried foods do not go bad. Packets of soup, potatoes
and milk powder are examples of dried foods. Meat
and fish are dried, in some parts of the world.
Explorers and mountaineers often take dried meat
on their expeditions, because it is lighter to carry
than tinned meat.

Dried foods are known as *dehydrated* foods.
You need to add water to dehydrated foods,
before you can eat them.

Food throughout the world

People in various parts of the world eat different foods.
In Britain, we eat lots of meat, bread and potatoes.
In Italy, people like foods made from flour paste,
such as pizza and spaghetti. In India and China,
the main food is rice.

In many parts of the world, large numbers of people
do not get enough to eat, so they become ill.
Many people also become ill, because they do not eat
a balanced diet. A person who becomes ill,
because he is not eating enough of the right foods,
is said to be suffering from *malnutrition*.

The diagram shows the differences between the diet
of a person living in Britain, and the diet of a person
living in India. The diagram compares the average amount
of each type of food, which is available to adults
in India and Britain each day. Unfortunately, many people
especially in India, eat far less than this.

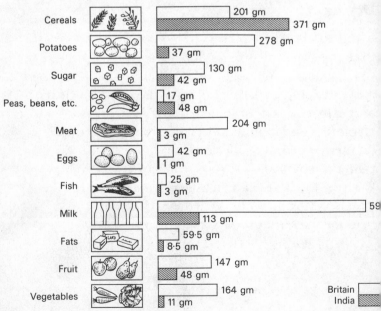

Food	Britain	India
Cereals	201 gm	371 gm
Potatoes	278 gm	37 gm
Sugar	130 gm	42 gm
Peas, beans, etc.	17 gm	48 gm
Meat	204 gm	3 gm
Eggs	42 gm	1 gm
Fish	25 gm	3 gm
Milk	59	113 gm
Fats	59·5 gm	8·5 gm
Fruit	147 gm	48 gm
Vegetables	164 gm	11 gm

Famines and food shortages

Sometimes, all the people living in a particular area
have no food at all to eat, and so they starve.
This is called a *famine*. All the crops may be ruined
in a flood, or there may be a very bad harvest.
No rain may fall in that area for months – or even years!
There may be a war which ruins the farmland.

When a famine occurs, organisations like Oxfam
send help. The picture shows food being prepared
for hungry people at a feeding centre in Somalia in 1981.

Food shortages

A food shortage occurs when an area has some food, but not enough to go round. There is always a food shortage after a famine.

In many countries, food shortages occur because the farming methods do not produce enough food. Large organisations, such as Freedom from Hunger and Oxfam, give some help by setting up projects to improve the methods of farming. Rich countries sometimes give aid to poor countries, by sending them money, machines and grain. The United Nations tries to improve the world food supply by using the Food and Agricultural Organisation, which has its headquarters in Rome.

Even so, the poor countries of the world are always in need of help. In the world, one person in every three still does not get enough of the right foods to eat each day.

These men are learning the proper methods of weeding and caring for coffee seedlings.

Glossary

calorie (p. 4) a measure of the amount of energy produced by a certain type of food

carbohydrates (p. 6) substances found in many foods, which help to provide the body with energy; they contain carbon and hydrogen, as well as oxygen.

dehydrate (p. 19) to remove all the water from something

diet (p. 13) (1) a person's usual food and drink (2) a special selection of food and drink which a person makes in order to stay healthy or to slim

digestion (p. 15) the way in which the body changes food into a form that it can use

enzymes (p. 15) chemical substances found in living cells which help to change one substance into another

famine (p. 21) a very serious shortage of food in some parts of the world

kilojoule (p. 4) a unit used in science to measure energy

malnutrition (p. 20) the poor state of health which comes when people do not eat enough food, or eat the wrong kind of food

oesophagus (p. 15) the food tube which runs from the throat to the stomach

preserve (food) (p. 19) to treat food in a special way, so that it can be kept in good condition for a long time

proteins (p. 7) substances found in many animal and vegetable products, which help to make new cells for the body, and to keep it healthy

vitamins (p. 8) chemical substances found in certain foods in very small amounts, which help to keep you healthy

First published 1982 by
Edward Arnold (Publishers) Ltd
41 Bedford Square
London WC1B 3DQ

Edward Arnold (Australia) Pty Ltd
80 Waverley Road, Caulfield East
Victoria 3145, Australia

Reprinted 1986

British Library Cataloguing in Publication Data
Crystal, David
    Food.—(Databank)
    1. Food
    I. Title   II. Foster, John L. (John Louis)
    III. Series
    641.3 TX354

    ISBN 0–7131–0631–X

Acknowledgements
The Publishers would like to thank the following for permission
to reproduce copyright photographs:
Iain Reid: Cover;
Antony McAvoy: p1 (Flashmans of Lordship Lane, SE22), 3l;
J. Allan Cash Ltd: 3r;
Courtesy of Wellcome Museum of Medical Science: pp 8, 9t & b;
St. Bartholomew's Hospital: 9c;
Barnaby's Picture Library: p 10;
Henry Grant: p 12;
Weight Watchers (UK) Ltd: p 13;
Oxfam: pp 21, 22.

Text set in 12/14 pt Baskerville by Oxprint Ltd, Oxford and
printed by photolithography in Great Britain at The Bath
Press, Avon